POEMS BY:
WENDI LOU STEELE

ILLUSTRATIONS BY: CADE SIEMERS

The Enchanting

Mrs. Hattie Pence

To Emily —
Blessings!
Wendi Lou Steele

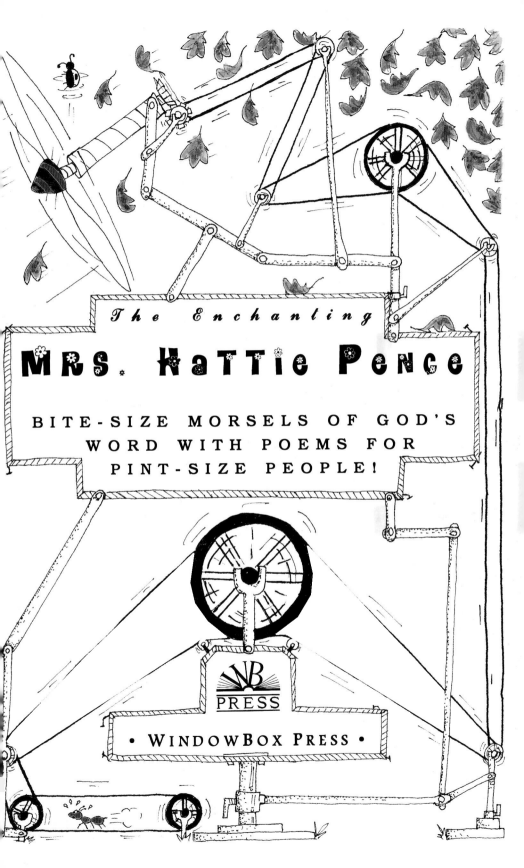

The Enchanting

MRS. HATTIE PENCE

BITE-SIZE MORSELS OF GOD'S WORD WITH POEMS FOR PINT-SIZE PEOPLE!

WB
PRESS

• WINDOWBOX PRESS •

THE ENCHANTING MRS. HATTIE PENCE

Text copyright © 1998 by Wendi Lou Steele.
Illustrations copyright © 1998 by WINDOWBOX PRESS.

First edition 1998

Library of Congress Catalog Card Number: 97-91016
Steele, Wendi Lou
The Enchanting Mrs. Hattie Pence:
Bite-Size Morsels of God's Word
With Poems for Pint-Size People/
by Wendi Lou Steele; illustrated by Cade Siemers
p. 96 cm.
Summary: An illustrated collection of biblical verses
and original poems for children.
ISBN 0-9660868-0-5
1. Children's poetry. (1.Poetry - Collections.)
I. Steele, Wendi L. (Wendi Lou)
II. Siemers, Cade, ill.   III Title.

Printed and bound in Korea.

"And the seed in the good soil,
these are the ones who have heard the word
in an honest and good heart, and hold it fast ... "
Luke 8:15 NASB

Published by

PRESS

• WINDOWBOX PRESS •
• P.O. Box 1035 •
• Great Falls, VA 22066•

Dedicated to our little
Miss Madison MacKensey

PREFACE

"SEEK FROM THE BOOK OF THE LORD, AND READ . . . "
ISAIAH 34:16

With skinny arms wrapped around equally spiny legs, I remember hunkering down on our front porch one sticky August afternoon shortly after turning the important age of eight. I suppose most kids didn't notice that this particular day of summer vacation was any different from all of the others, but it was indeed! This was *the* very particular day that a certain eight year old had a *very* important conversation with God.

Grownups might call this conversation a "soliloquy" – since my job was to do all of the talking solo while God's part was being *the* Most Interested Listener. But since He actually did a much better job listening than I did talking about things eight year olds don't know too much about, it only seems fair that both of us be counted when remembering that particular summer day.

Our conversation was about my believing whether or not God was who He said He was – which was really a combination of who parents, Sunday School teachers and other grownups told me who He was.   Now that I was eight, it seemed particularly important that I decide for myself, by myself, just what believing in God was all about.

The problem, I explained to God, was that His Word -- the Bible -- was awfully complicated and often rather confusing for an eight year old from Pennsylvania.   And though "children's Bibles" had pictures, which always made reading *anything* easier and more fun, the words were different than His Word -- which simply made the kids' version little more than colorful stories told by grownups I didn't even know. That was the problem.

It was an important day because I decided to read His Word anyway -- the grownup version -- by myself.   I did suggest that since He was both God and the Most Interested Listener, perhaps He would help me understand just what He wanted me to know about Himself -- especially since grownups didn't see fit to include pictures in His especially long Book, and thus I might need more than a little help paying attention.

Once again it is an August afternoon, and so many birthdays have passed that neither my arms nor my legs would qualify as "spiny" to even the most visually challenged among us. As a new parent on this particular day, it seems *very* important to help fix the problem our little Miss Madison MacKensey may have when she turns the important age of eight.   There will be several summers before she can hunker down on the front porch and read about the enchanting Mrs. Hattie Pence and her friends, but since I am still trying to understand just what God wants me to know about Himself through His Word, I am most interested in getting a particularly early start.

Thank you for joining us on this most important adventure.

CONTENTS

EACH ONE HAS RECEIVED A SPECIAL GIFT,

EMPLOY IT IN SERVING ONE ANOTHER . . .

I PETER 4:10

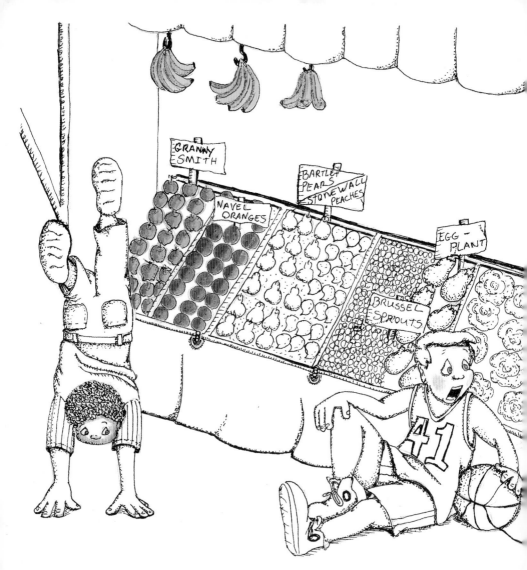

MRS. HATTIE PENCE

Samuel is mighty --
    His arms are muscular and strong.
Jonathan is swift --
    His legs are very lean and long.
Samuel can carry heavy loads
    but not too far.
Jonathan can run forever
    like a sleek jaguar.

Samuel & Jonathan observed
just by coincidence
An incident of consequence
regarding Mrs. Hattie Pence.

The wind was very gusty
and without any forewarning
It captured Hattie Pence's hat
just as she said, "Good Morning!"

11.

She watched in helpless worry
    as it blew end-over-end.
Since her arms were filled with groceries
    she had no way to apprehend
Her hat -- her lovely hat! --
    What was Hattie Pence to do?
That's when Samuel and Jonathan
    came to Hattie's quick rescue.

MARKET AV.

Jon dashed down the avenue
 and captured Hattie's hat
While Sam gathered her groceries --
 balancing like an acrobat.
The boys escorted Hattie home
 each serving with his gift.
Their friendship complementary:
 Sam is mighty --
 Jon is swift.

HOLY AND AWESOME IS HIS NAME.

PSALM 111:9

MAKIN' BREEZES

God's name is enormously holy
But nothing like Swiss cheese.
It means He's even more special
Than a kite is to a breeze.

God's name is especially awesome!
For I have never met a man
Who can sneeze, like God, and make a breeze.
God's the only One Who can!

15.

SET YOUR MIND ON THE THINGS ABOVE, NOT ON THE THINGS THAT ARE ON EARTH.

COLOSSIANS 3:2

TUCKED IN

When Benjamin is tucked in bed
  his head is full of worry.
For underneath his sheets Ben is
  convinced there is a furry Beast
With jagged teeth and bloodshot eyes,
  and, worse, there's more:
Ben thinks the Beast is hungry!
  Ben can't sleep and that's for sure!

16.

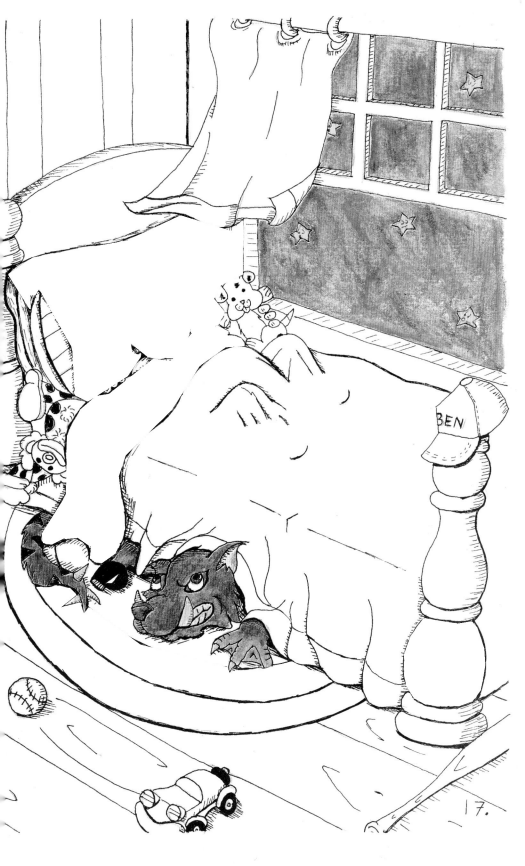

18.

Ben has a twin, named Ken,
 and when he's tucked in bed he's fine.
Ken likes to look into the heavens
 and count all the stars that shine.
Then Ken pretends he's flying with
 an angel to the moon.
Ken is convinced no furry Beasts
 are living in their room!

19.

THEREFORE EVERYONE WHO HEARS THESE WORDS OF MINE, AND ACTS UPON THEM, MAY BE COMPARED TO A WISE MAN, WHO BUILT HIS HOUSE UPON THE ROCK. AND THE RAIN DESCENDED, AND THE FLOODS CAME, AND THE WINDS BLEW, AND BURST AGAINST THAT HOUSE; AND YET IT DID NOT FALL, FOR IT HAD BEEN FOUNDED UPON THE ROCK. AND EVERYONE WHO HEARS THESE WORDS OF MINE, AND DOES NOT ACT UPON THEM, WILL BE LIKE A FOOLISH MAN, WHO BUILT HIS HOUSE UPON THE SAND. AND THE RAIN DESCENDED, AND THE FLOODS CAME, AND THE WINDS BLEW, AND BURST AGAINST THAT HOUSE; AND IT FELL, AND GREAT WAS ITS FALL.

MATTHEW 7:24-27

20.

HOME IMPROVEMENTS

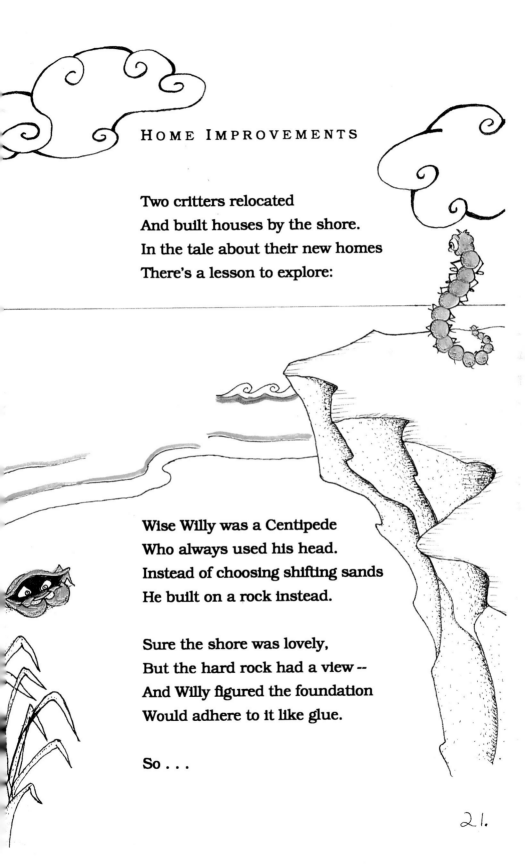

Two critters relocated
And built houses by the shore.
In the tale about their new homes
There's a lesson to explore:

Wise Willy was a Centipede
Who always used his head.
Instead of choosing shifting sands
He built on a rock instead.

Sure the shore was lovely,
But the hard rock had a view --
And Willy figured the foundation
Would adhere to it like glue.

So . . .

Willy went to work
Using all his hundred legs –
Some sawed the wooden branches,
Others hammered wooden pegs.

22.

After six long days
Wise Willy's home was done –
And he walked his hundred weary feet
Down to the beach to sun.

That's where Willy found
His new neighbor, Frank the fool.
For Frank was a Blue Crab
With the dull sense of a mule.

Stubborn and shortsighted,
Frank had built his fragile home
With tiny twigs and slimy seaweed
Just beyond the ocean's foam.

His claws had scrambled quickly
And completed in just one day
The residence of Frank the Crab –
Then to the sand, he went to play!

One dark evening soon thereafter,
When the critters were in their beds
A fierce sea storm descended
With pelting rain and thunder-heads.

The tide began to rise
And the ferocious winds blew.
It flooded Frank the Crab's whole home,
Soaking all his belongings, too!

Meanwhile . . .

24.

Willy was loudly snoring,
Snug and dry in his new place.
He had build his seaside home for storms
Because such weather's commonplace.

At dawn . . .

25.

Frank's shabby home was left in shambles,
While Willy's was safe upon the rock.
This tale made Willy a local legend and
Foolish Frank a laughingstock!

WHAT IS MAN, THAT THOU REMEMBEREST HIM? OR THE SON OF MAN THAT THOU ART CONCERNED ABOUT HIM? THOU HAST MADE HIM FOR A LITTLE WHILE LOWER THAN THE ANGELS . . .

HEBREWS 2:6-7

GUS MEETS GRAVITY

God made Gus a little lower than the angels.
This he knows because he surely can't fly.
Every time Gus leaps off a lounge chair
His feet hit the patio, not the sky.

 JOYFUL HEART, MAKES A CHEERFUL FACE,

BUT WHEN THE HEART IS SAD, THE SPIRIT IS BROKEN.

PROVERBS 15:13

28.

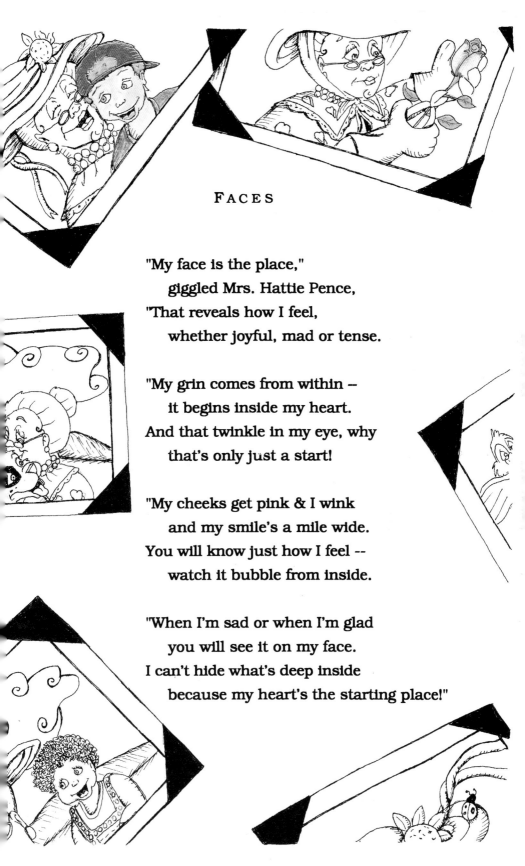

FACES

"My face is the place,"
   giggled Mrs. Hattie Pence,
"That reveals how I feel,
   whether joyful, mad or tense.

"My grin comes from within –
   it begins inside my heart.
And that twinkle in my eye, why
   that's only just a start!

"My cheeks get pink & I wink
   and my smile's a mile wide.
You will know just how I feel --
   watch it bubble from inside.

"When I'm sad or when I'm glad
   you will see it on my face.
I can't hide what's deep inside
   because my heart's the starting place!"

FOR HE WILL GIVE HIS ANGELS

CHARGE CONCERNING YOU,

TO GUARD YOU IN ALL YOUR WAYS.

THEY WILL BEAR YOU UP IN THEIR HANDS,

LEST YOU STRIKE YOUR FOOT AGAINST A STONE.

PSALM 91:11-12

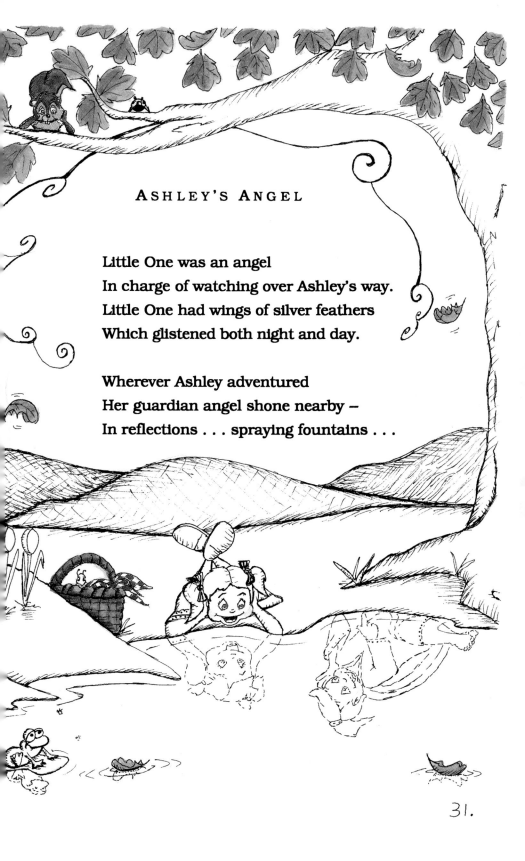

ASHLEY'S ANGEL

Little One was an angel
In charge of watching over Ashley's way.
Little One had wings of silver feathers
Which glistened both night and day.

Wherever Ashley adventured
Her guardian angel shone nearby –
In reflections . . . spraying fountains . . .

And in the twilight sky.

Ashley knew her Little One
Was sent by God above
To protect her from unseen dangers --
His angels are a special gift of love!

WHAT MAN AMONG YOU, IF HE HAS A HUNDRED SHEEP AND HAS LOST ONE OF THEM, DOES NOT LEAVE THE NINETY-NINE IN THE OPEN PASTURE, AND GO AFTER THE ONE WHICH IS LOST, UNTIL HE FINDS IT? AND WHEN HE HAS FOUND IT, HE LAYS IT ON HIS SHOULDERS, REJOICING.

LUKE 15:4-5

33.

100 WOOLLY ONES

One Sheep, two Sheep,
Count six more --
Do that three times
And there's twenty-four.

34.

Shepherds keep track
Of every woolly one --
Add another seven
That's thirty-one.
Ten more on my left
And nine on my right.
Must keep counting
To know my flock's alright.

Now I'm at fifty,
I'm halfway through.
There's twelve more sheep --
I have counted sixty-two.
Down in the pasture
More have gathered for a chat --
I'm now up to eighty-four
Just like that!

36.

And there by the stream
Sipping snugly in a line,
I count fifteen more --
Now I'm up to ninety-nine.

Where is my last Sheep?
I've looked left and right --
Climbed to the hilltop,
She's nowhere in sight.
I must leave the pasture
To find my little Lamb.
Where she might have wandered
I don't yet understand.

"A ha!" rejoiced the Shepherd,
"She's napping near the rock.
I found my lost woolly one,
Now I've counted my whole flock!"

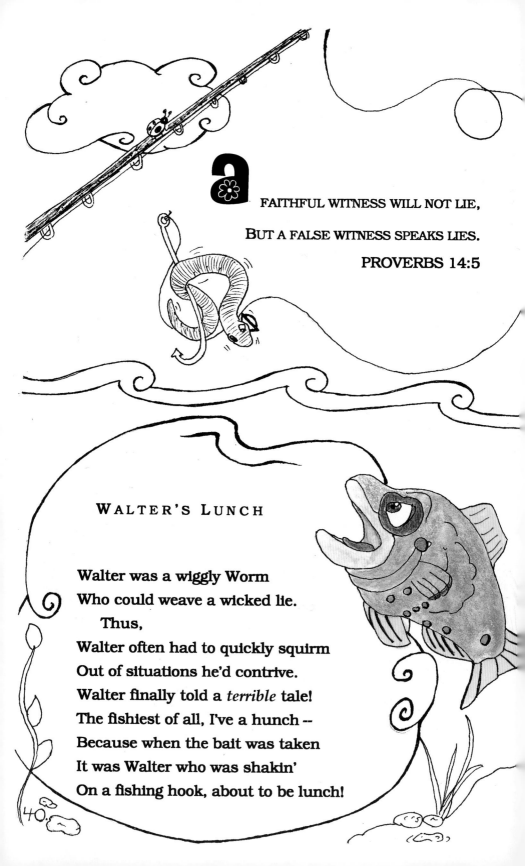

A FAITHFUL WITNESS WILL NOT LIE,

BUT A FALSE WITNESS SPEAKS LIES.

PROVERBS 14:5

WALTER'S LUNCH

Walter was a wiggly Worm
Who could weave a wicked lie.
   Thus,
Walter often had to quickly squirm
Out of situations he'd contrive.
Walter finally told a *terrible* tale!
The fishiest of all, I've a hunch --
Because when the bait was taken
It was Walter who was shakin'
On a fishing hook, about to be lunch!

LOVE IS PATIENT, LOVE IS KIND, & IS NOT JEALOUS; LOVE DOES NOT BRAG AND IS NOT ARROGANT, DOES NOT ACT UNBECOMINGLY; IT DOES NOT SEEK ITS OWN, IS NOT PROVOKED, DOES NOT TAKE INTO ACCOUNT A WRONG SUFFERED, DOES NOT REJOICE IN UNRIGHTEOUSNESS, BUT REJOICES WITH THE TRUTH; BEARS ALL THINGS, BELIEVES ALL THINGS, HOPES ALL THINGS, ENDURES ALL THINGS. LOVE NEVER FAILS !

I CORINTHIANS 13:4-8

41.

SNUGGLES

Some say love is snuggles
Or Puppy Dogs
Or blind --

I know love is patient,
Never jealous,
Always kind.

Some say love is roses
Or a dance
Or simply living --

I know love is modest,
Never selfish,
Always forgiving.

Some say love is friendship
  Or a cookie
    Or a Bear --

I know love is truthful,
  Never burdened,
    Always fair.

Some say love is scary
  Or too risky
    Or untrue --

I know love is faithful,
  Never doubting,
    Just like you.

43.

LOVE DOES NO WRONG TO A NEIGHBOR;

LOVE THEREFORE IS THE FULFILLMENT OF THE LAW.

ROMANS 13:10

LOVELY AND LOUSY NEIGHBORS

Willy is a splendid friend
And much loved by his neighbors.
He offers to help with all of his legs --
Willy works and toils and labors.

Some Crabs in town just lounge around
Never lifting a claw to share.
They gossip and chat, and mischief like that --
If they moved, the neighbors wouldn't care!

44.

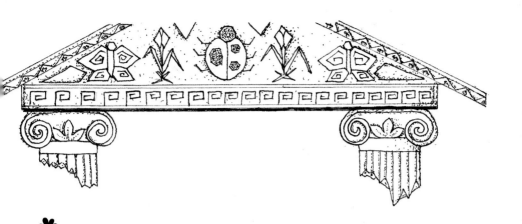

ESUS REPLIED AND SAID, "A CERTAIN MAN WAS GOING DOWN FROM JERUSALEM TO JERICHO; AND HE FELL AMONG ROBBERS, AND THEY STRIPPED HIM AND BEAT HIM, AND WENT OFF LEAVING HIM HALF DEAD. AND BY CHANCE A CERTAIN PRIEST WAS GOING DOWN ON THAT ROAD, AND WHEN HE SAW HIM, HE PASSED BY ON THE OTHER SIDE. AND LIKEWISE A LEVITE ALSO, WHEN HE CAME TO THE PLACE AND SAW HIM, PASSED BY ON THE OTHER SIDE. BUT A CERTAIN SAMARITAN, WHO WAS ON A JOURNEY, CAME UPON HIM; AND WHEN HE SAW HIM, HE FELT COMPASSION, AND CAME TO HIM, AND BANDAGED UP HIS WOUNDS, POURING OIL AND WINE ON THEM; AND HE PUT HIM ON HIS OWN BEAST, AND BROUGHT HIM TO AN INN, AND TOOK CARE OF HIM."

LUKE 10:30-34

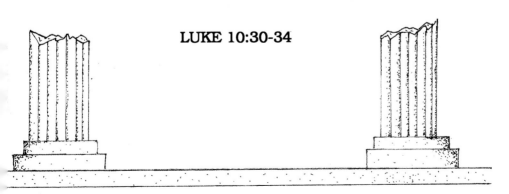

45.

JERICHO →

Jake was on a journey
　　from Jerusalem to Jericho
　　　　when he ran into some bad dudes,
　　　　　　some mean and nasty rude dudes,
Who beat him up and left him there half-dead.

A pompous Priest was passing
　　down the same ol' road to Jericho.
　　　　He saw Jake's battered body
　　　　　　but the priest was cold and haughty
And selfishly he crossed the road instead.

Then Levi the Levite ambled
     down the same ol' road to Jericho.
          He noticed Jake was bleeding,
               needing help and pleading,
But Levi just walked by and turned his head.

Finally . . .

47.

Fred the Samaritan
was on the same ol' road to Jericho.
He saw Jake and felt compassion,
fixed him up with Band-Aid fashion
And took Jake to an inn to rest in bed.

If you ever journey
down the same ol' road to Jericho
beware of meeting bad dudes,
and priests and others who, too, are rude,
But bless all good Samaritans like Fred.

49.

MAKE FOR YOURSELF AN ARK . . . .

AND OF EVERY LIVING THING OF ALL FLESH, YOU SHALL BRING TWO OF EVERY KIND INTO THE ARK, TO KEEP THEM ALIVE WITH YOU; THEY SHALL BE MALE AND FEMALE. OF THE BIRDS . . . AND OF THE ANIMALS . . . OF EVERY CREEPING THING OF THE GROUND . . . TWO OF EVERY KIND SHALL COME TO YOU TO KEEP THEM ALIVE.

AND NOAH DID ACCORDING TO ALL THAT THE LORD HAD COMMANDED HIM. . . . THE FLOOD OF WATER CAME UPON THE EARTH. AND THE RAIN FELL UPON THE EARTH FOR FORTY DAYS AND FORTY NIGHTS.

GENESIS 6:14, 19-20 AND 7:5-6, 12

50.

ONE ARK, TWO LARKS
AND
A BOAT LOAD OF FRIENDS

God told Noah to build an ark
    to float upon the flooded sea of blue
And to fill that wooden hull to the brim
    with species two-by-two.

Two Bears and two Turtles
    and two Bunny Rabbits, too;
Camels and Larks and lanky Aardvarks
    and hopping Kangaroos.

51.

Then the rains came and it rained and rained
and rained and rained some more,
But Noah and his furry and feathered friends
stayed cozy, dry and warm.

Noah and the animals stayed safe from the flood
in a wooden ark quite grand --
But Noah would have been all washed up
if he hadn't first listened to God's command!

H E MADE THE MOON FOR THE SEASONS;

THE SUN KNOWS THE PLACE OF ITS SETTING.

THOU DOST APPOINT DARKNESS

AND IT BECOMES NIGHT,

IN WHICH ALL THE BEASTS OF THE FOREST

PROWL ABOUT.

PSALM 104:19-20

SUN DANCE AND MOON WALK

I wonder how the sun wakes up
Outside my window every day.
It knows when I'm at home
Or at my Grandma's house to stay.

And late in the afternoons
Every place I play,
The sun dances down beyond the yard
Just before the sky goes gray.

54.

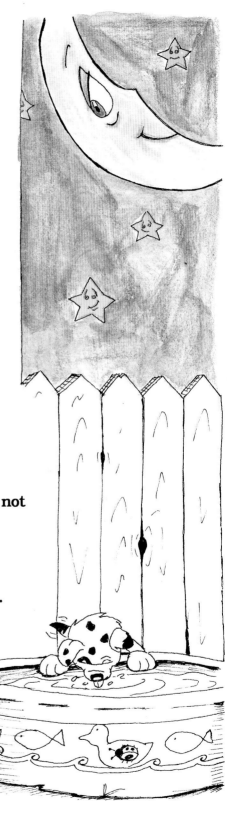

I wonder how the moon wakes up
Outside my window every night.
Sometimes it's full and sometimes not
Still it always shines so bright.

It knows when I'm at home
Or at my Grandpa's house to stay.
I'd like to ask the moon sometime
If he's met the sun along the way.

SING TO THE LORD A NEW SONG.

SING TO THE LORD, ALL THE EARTH.

PSALM 96:1

KRISTEN'S NIFTY NEW SONG

Kristen is singing a new song.
It goes:
"Fa - la,
   Tee - hee,
Fa -
   la -
      low!"

She sings it while bouncing
   on her trampoline
And every other place she goes.

"Fa - la,
   Tee - hee,
Fa -
   la -
      low!
I'm singing a tune for today.
To the Birds above
   and my Buttons below,
I'm singing a nifty new song
   which goes:
Fa - la,
   Tee - hee,
Fa -
   la -
      low!"

AND THE LORD BLESSED

THE LATTER DAYS OF JOB

MORE THAN HIS BEGINNING,

AND HE HAD 14,000 SHEEP,

AND 6,000 CAMELS,

AND 1,000 YOKE OF OXEN,

AND 1,000 FEMALE DONKEYS.

JOB 42:12

JOB'S 22,000 BARNYARD BLESSINGS

There was a guy named Job
    (that rhymes with "earlobe") –
This Job had a very hard life.

But he never stopped believing,
    in spite of years of grieving –
Job trusted God even in strife.

59.

Job was then richly blessed
    (because his faith stood the test)
Soon his life became quite a zoo –

God gave him Camels to keep,
    thousands of woolly Sheep,
And Oxen and Donkeys, too!

BUT THOSE WHO WANT TO GET RICH

FALL INTO TEMPTATION AND A SNARE

AND MANY FOOLISH AND HARMFUL DESIRES

WHICH PLUNGE MEN INTO RUIN AND DESTRUCTION.

FOR THE LOVE OF MONEY

IS A ROOT OF ALL SORTS OF EVIL . . .

I TIMOTHY 6:9-10

A HARE SNARE

Funny Barrett Bunny
Cared more about money
Than making his Honey Bunny happy.

He wrote jokes all day
And every evening he'd play
At The Maple Tree Club dubbed "Sappy's."

He'd hop onto the stage
And cleverly engage
The crowd 'til there were roars of laughter.

He'd gather his pay
Which grew day after day
But Honey Bunny always came after

> *The money!*
> *The money!*
> Barrett's large mounds of money.

Everyone thought
That her Barrett was funny --

Except lonely Honey Bunny,
The saddest Bunny in town.

'Cause no amount of money
62. Can turn a frown upside down.

HEN I AM AFRAID, I WILL PUT MY TRUST IN THEE.

IN GOD, WHOSE WORD I PRAISE,
IN GOD I HAVE PUT MY TRUST;
I SHALL NOT BE AFRAID.
PSALM 56:3-4

BIG-TIME FEAR

Ben is afraid of furry beasts.
Gus declares nothing will do him harm.
But Amanda, she's afraid big-time
   of growing an extra arm.

Some may say Amanda's silly.
Others find her fear quite odd.
But Amanda knows that no fear is too small
   or big-time to trust to God.

OH LORD, HOW MANY ARE THY WORKS!

IN WISDOM, THOU HAS MADE THEM ALL;

THE EARTH IS FULL OF THY POSSESSIONS.

THERE IS THE SEA, GREAT AND BROAD,

IN WHICH ARE SWARMS WITHOUT NUMBER,

ANIMALS BOTH SMALL AND GREAT

THERE THE SHIPS MOVE ALONG . . .

PSALM 104:24-26

65.

CARIBBEAN WAVE

She is a Caribbean wave
    rolling on the sea so great and broad.
The wonders of the salty world
    make her swell with thanks to God.
She carries boats upon her back
    as they catch the island breeze
While below swim schools of Angel Fish
    and Turtles of the sea.

Together swarms of vibrant creatures
    dart around a reef
That decorates the sandy floor
    with coral castles far beneath.
She loves to uplift people
    and hold the fish under her foam.
How many are Thy works, she gushes,
    in my Caribbean home!

HAPPY BIRTHDAY

BEHOLD, CHILDREN ARE A GIFT OF THE LORD . . .

PSALM 127:3

THE PERFECT PRESENT

Mrs. Hattie Pence is having a birthday.
She isn't turning twelve or ten or five --
In fact, none of the kids in the neighborhood
Know just how many years she's been alive!

Everyone has brought her a present --
Ken colored a card to hang on the fridge.
Gus picked a bouquet of dandelions
And Amanda made a deck of cards for bridge.

Mrs. Hattie Pence so loves her surprises!
Her party . . . and presents . . . and cake.
But the best gift of all
   arrived both tall and quite small --
Her friends for the laughter they make!

YOU SHALL NOT STEAL.

EXODUS 20:15

B. Naughtingham

B. NAUGHTINGHAM

B. Naughtingham was a Squirrel
Who resided in a lush condo tree
With six other squirrelly neighbors
Who nicknamed him "B. Naughty."

Because B. Naughtingham had a habit
That wasn't very neighborly at all:
He'd sneak into the six other units
And steal all their acorns -- *What gall!*

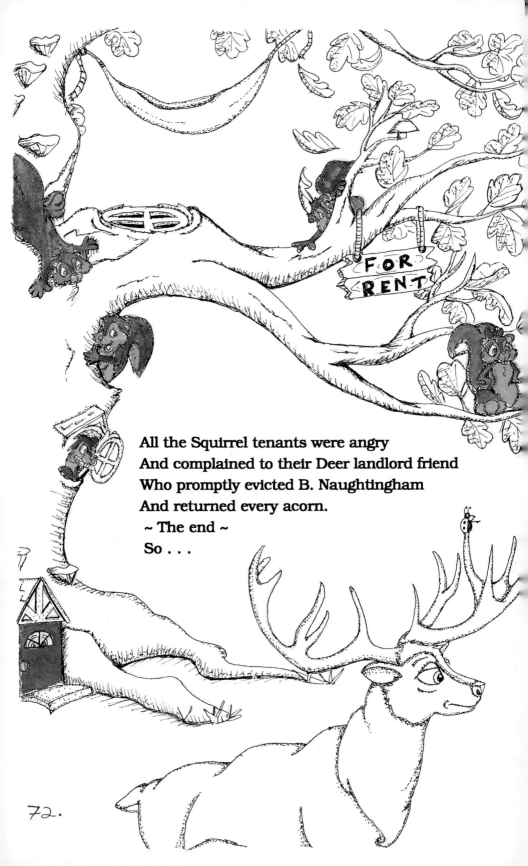

All the Squirrel tenants were angry
And complained to their Deer landlord friend
Who promptly evicted B. Naughtingham
And returned every acorn.
 ~ The end ~
 So . . .

The moral of the Squirrel's tale is simple:
If you steal other's acorns you are nuts!
You too would B. Naughty and unneighborly
Because nobody at all likes a putz.

A CONSTANT DRIPPING ON A DAY OF STEADY RAIN AND A CONTENTIOUS WOMAN ARE ALIKE.

PROVERBS 27:15

ALL WET

When I listen to somebody
Fuss and complain --

Their yammering sounds like
A day of steady rain.

Pitter-patter,
Pitter-patter.

Drip,
Drip,
Drip.

Beating on my ears
With a noise that won't quit.

Pitter-patter,
Pitter-patter.

Tap,
Tap,
Tap.

Constant whining.

Yap,
Yap,
Yap.

AND ALSO IF ANYONE COMPETES AS AN ATHLETE,
HE DOES NOT WIN THE PRIZE UNLESS HE COMPETES
ACCORDING TO THE RULES.

2 TIMOTHY 2:5

OCEAN OLYMPICS

Oliver is an ostentatious Octopus.
Patrick is an ocean-famous Platypus.
Both are much faster than all the rest of us
Who live off Australia beneath the sea.

Oliver is speedy on his many feet --
And since Oliver has eight of 'em he's hard to beat.
He has made it to the Olympic finals to compete
Against Patrick, the swiftest Platypus beneath the sea.

The Platypus is Oliver's only contender,
And since he won the title last, he's also the defender.
But Patrick has an injured paddle that is tender --
He surely hopes it's tough enough to win the race!

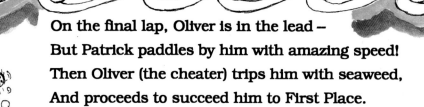

On the final lap, Oliver is in the lead –
But Patrick paddles by him with amazing speed!
Then Oliver (the cheater) trips him with seaweed,
And proceeds to succeed him to First Place.

Oliver ostentatiously takes a victory lap
While Patrick sits befuddled in the seaweed trap.
Then the Referee announces, "There's been a big mishap!
It seems our Octopus has cheated terribly!"

Oliver's afternoon went into quick demise

When the Referee took back his Olympic prize.

Patrick was declared the Winner, to his great surprise --

While all sea creatures cheered,

    "Fastest beneath the sea!"

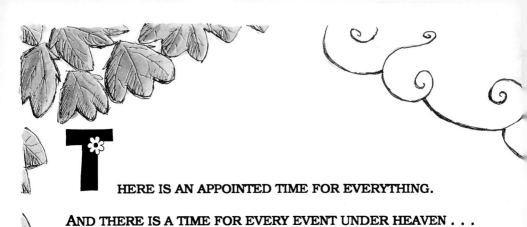

THERE IS AN APPOINTED TIME FOR EVERYTHING.

AND THERE IS A TIME FOR EVERY EVENT UNDER HEAVEN . . .

ECCLESIASTES 3:1-2

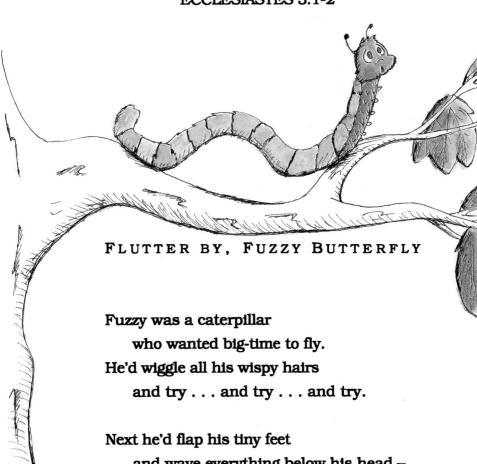

FLUTTER BY, FUZZY BUTTERFLY

Fuzzy was a caterpillar
    who wanted big-time to fly.
He'd wiggle all his wispy hairs
    and try . . . and try . . . and try.

Next he'd flap his tiny feet
    and wave everything below his head --
But no matter how hard Fuzzy'd try
    he stayed on the tree's limb instead.

So Fuzzy stopped to rest one day
  and curled up into a ball --
And before he knew it, Fuzzy'd spun
  a cocoon that covered all

Of Fuzzy's legs and Fuzzy's feet
  and Fuzzy's tummy, too.
Every part of Fuzzy's self
  was tucked in his cocoon.

And when there came a time for
    Fuzzy's big wish to come true:
He grew kite-colored wings
    inside his tight bright white cocoon.

In the Springtime Fuzzy awakened
    to discover his wonderful wings!
He flapped and fluttered, and mistakenly stuttered,
    "I'm a-a-a Flutterby, what a marvelous thing!"

Fuzzy's wings caught the Springtime air
    on the tree's limb which was *so* high
That he had no choice (to his delight)
    except to fly . . . and fly . . . and fly.

Flutter by,
Flutter by,
    there goes Fuzzy Butterfly!

a FOOL ALWAYS LOSES HIS TEMPER

BUT A WISE MAN HOLDS IT BACK.

PROVERBS 29:11

DAG-NABBIT, GOODNESS GRACIOUS

Darn!
   It seems I've lost my temper.
Phooey!
   I wonder where it could be?
Dang!
   Did I leave it in the market –
Shoot!
   When I became so angry?

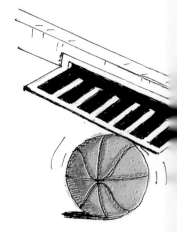

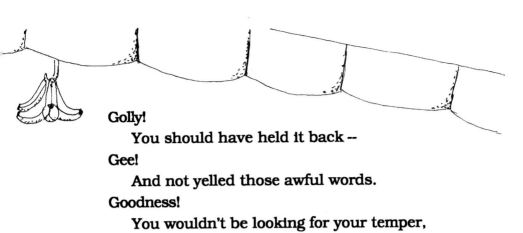

Golly!
> You should have held it back --

Gee!
> And not yelled those awful words.

Goodness!
> You wouldn't be looking for your temper,

Gracious!
> Which seems somewhat silly and absurd.

BUT NOW, O LORD, THOU ART OUR FATHER,

WE ARE THE CLAY, AND THOU OUR POTTER;

AND ALL OF US ARE THE WORK OF THY HAND.

ISAIAH 64:8

THE POTTER

The Potter is a warm old man
With understanding eyes --
   Deep and knowing
   Always showing
That His heart is kind and wise.

His hands are strong from years of work
With mounds of earthen clay.
   His fingers move
   To gently smooth
Each piece its perfect way.

Each work reflects the Potter's heart
And uniquely all portray
And glorify,
Like you and I,
The Potter of the clay.

87.

and let not your adornment be merely external . . . but let it be the hidden person of the heart, with the imperishable quality of a gentle and quiet spirit, which is precious in the sight of God.

I PETER 3:3-4

THE HERMIT

The Hermit Crab
   is admired by all

For his display of strength,
   even though he's really so small.

He marches about
   in his marvelous shell

But what he is inside
   you can't really tell.

For the amount of his flesh
   that shell's quite a burden.

And as the tides pass,
   it's bound to hurt him.

If he were to discard it
   one of these days

And you saw the real hermit
   you'd be quite amazed!

89.

T

HY WORD IS A LAMP TO MY FEET,

AND A LIGHT TO MY PATH.

PSALM 119:105

MOUNTAIN MAP

Life is like a summer camp hike
Through a wooded mountain pass.
There's abounding beauty to behold
Like rambling streams and sassafras.

90.

You see Birds and Bugs and Butterflies
And sometimes even Deer.
The presence of the wood's Creator
Often seems especially near!

But the path is sometimes overgrown --
It's hard not to lose your way.
There's poison oak and rains that soak
And dark shadows to lead you astray.

But God has given us his Word
To guide us like a lamp.
His wisdom's the best mountain map
To lead us safely back to camp.

I THANK MY GOD

IN ALL MY REMEMBRANCE OF YOU,
ALWAYS OFFERING PRAYER WITH JOY IN
MY EVERY PRAYER FOR YOU ALL . . . .
FOR IT IS ONLY RIGHT FOR ME TO FEEL
THIS WAY ABOUT YOU ALL, BECAUSE I
HAVE YOU IN MY HEART.

PHILLIPPIANS 1:3-7

TOODLE-OO!

For some of you it's time to nap –
  for others, time to say,
  "Night, night!"
If that's the case, my special Friend,
  I pray that you sleep tight.

Rest well, dear Child –
  dream enchanting dreams
  of life's wonders and love!
And know God's watching over you
  while His angels fly above.

Please say your prayers --
  and give thanks, dear Child,
  for His promises come true.
And know that you are in my prayers
  this day and tomorrow, too.

I'll see you in but a while, dear Child –
  so I bid farewell, 'til then.
Toodle-oo, Ciao-bye, and See you soon,
  my *very* special Friend!

95.

WENDI LOU STEELE is a former political appointee for presidents Ronald Reagan, George Bush and Bill Clinton. Alongside her love of conservative politics, Wendi is a popular inspirational writer and public speaker. Prior to her career in national service, Wendi was both a teacher and youth counselor. She and her husband Nick, and their precious blessing Miss Madison MacKensey, reside in McLean, Virginia.

CADE SIEMERS is a free-lance illustrator and actor having lived and performed in London. He is a graduate of TASIS England and The University of Texas at Austin. Presently, he is the technical theater director and drama teacher at Leander High School where he has designed sets for and produced numerous acclaimed performances. His residence is Austin, Texas.